ISBN 978-1-332-10655-4
PIBN 10285498

1 MONTH OF
FREE
READING

at

www.ForgottenBooks.com

By purchasing this book you are eligible for one month membership to ForgottenBooks.com, giving you unlimited access to our entire collection of over 700,000 titles via our web site and mobile apps.

To claim your free month visit:

www.forgottenbooks.com/free285498

English
Français
Deutsche
Italiano
Español
Português

www.forgottenbooks.com

Mythology Photography **Fiction**
Fishing Christianity **Art** Cooking
Essays Buddhism Freemasonry
Medicine **Biology** Music **Ancient**
Egypt Evolution Carpentry Physics
Dance Geology **Mathematics** Fitness
Shakespeare **Folklore** Yoga Marketing
Confidence Immortality Biographies
Poetry **Psychology** Witchcraft
Electronics Chemistry History **Law**
Accounting **Philosophy** Anthropology
Alchemy Drama Quantum Mechanics
Atheism Sexual Health **Ancient History**
Entrepreneurship Languages Sport
Paleontology Needlework Islam
Metaphysics Investment Archaeology
Parenting Statistics Criminology
Motivational

SEE FRONTISPIECE.

The mink, from head to tail, is usually 15 to 18 inches long. The tail is about half as long as the body, making the entire length from 22 to 27 inches.

The female is smaller than the male. The ears are rounded, small and nearly hidden by the adjacent fur. The fur is soft and thick, Mixed with long, lustrous hairs on all parts of the body and tail. The tail is rather bushy but slightly tapering at the end. Northern mink have the finest and glossiest fur, which is of a rich, dark brown color; the back being the darker and the tail nearly black. The head is broad and there is a white spot on the under jaw.

CHAPTER I.

INTRODUCTION

In this book the writer intends to illustrate the practical side of mink raising, and to show how easily mink may be made to net their owner from $50 to $5,000 or more each year.

It is our intention to give the reader practical advice and instruction as to the securing, breeding and marketing of mink; being the result of experience, observation and consultation with other mink breeders.

Of all the small fur-bearing animals in this section, the mink is the most valuable, bringing as much as $8 for prime, dark mink, and there is reason to believe that within the next two years the price will advance to $12 or more. For breeding purposes they were bringing $25 each, as reported by Mr. W. G. Gates of Idaho, in March, 1913.

The catch of mink is steadily decreasing, the price is steadily advancing, and it will not be long before the best mink pelts will bring the price quoted in the preceding paragraph, and a pair of fine breeders will probably bring as much as $75.

Fur breeding is just beginning to attract attention. The ever increasing trapping information has made it possible for a greater number each year to catch our fur animals, and the ranks of the fur bearers are rapidly being thinned out.

There is a catch of probably $15,000,000 worth of fur yearly, at trappers' prices, and while the demand for fur is increasing, if the fur bearers are being thinned out, how is that demand to be supplied? The answer is breed and raise the fur. That seems the only answer, and it is really necessary therefore that mink farming be taken up as a business in order to perpetuate its luxurious fur.

Furs are a necessary luxury; the market can never be oversupplied; the future of fur farming is secure. The United States Government is experimenting in mink farming and there are indications that the mink industry will soon be taken up by many. Those who are already in the business and have stock to sell for breeding purposes will reap the reward for being ready. Before many years a farm stocked with 100 female mink should bring the owner, during the following December, an income of over $8,000.

CHAPTER II.

EXPERIENCE

"Our first mink farm," writes Mr. J. B. Smith, a well-known Pennsylvania trapper, "was on a small sandy island in the west branch of the Susquehanna River and the stock consisted of a pair of wild mink, which were seen one afternoon in the early spring of 1898 digging at a hole in the sandy bank of the island.

"A great deal of spare time was spent in the vicinity of this island, either in the canoe or on the bank at a safe distance from the den, and one evening, about the middle of May, six young mink were seen at play near the mouth of the den.

"A peculiar fact about this family of mink was that, although the mink while in captivity do not pair and the male will kill the young, still this pair lived in the same den with their young until June, when the whole family was dug out and put in a large dry-goods box.

"The den or hole in which the mink were found was about nine feet long, terminating in a room or nest, which was lined with fine dry grass.

"Later in the summer a 5-foot strip on the upper floor of our barn, which was 30 feet wide, was divided into pens 5 feet square, with connecting doors between, and we began to wean the mink from an all-meat diet to one of milk and cornmeal.

"The young mink made the change quite readily, but the old pair were very wild and savage, and for a long time would not eat much of the milk and cornmeal. They were given as many sparrows as could be caught for them, and they gradually acquired a taste for the cornmeal mush.

"About the middle of the following December, when their fur was prime, the old male and the two young males were killed and their pelts marketed. A new male, caught that winter, was placed with the five females.

"Having had several years' experience in breeding ferrets, we raised the mink in the same way, and in the following May had two dozen young mink. Twenty of these lived, and when their fur was prime, three of the darkest young females were saved with the two darkest old females and the male, and the rest were killed and marketed, clearing us about $75 over the cost of raising them.

"At the present time those 17 young and 3 old mink would bring about $150 as fur, and for breeding purposes would sell for $500 at the present prices."

CHAPTER III.

THE FARM

The "farm" or pen may be a box not smaller than 4 or 5 feet square and 3 feet high. Across the lower two-thirds of the front should be stretched a 1-inch wire mesh 2 feet wide, leaving the upper third of the box boarded. A hinged cover 2 feet wide should be placed across the top in front,

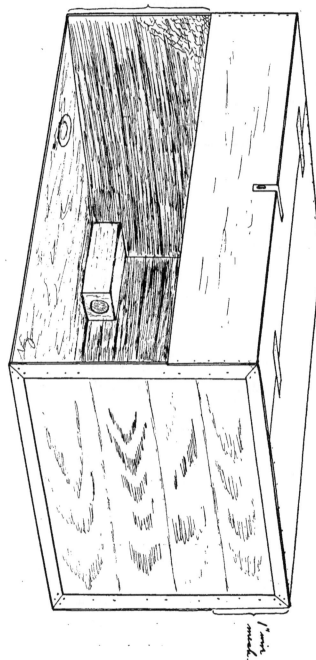

Fig. 1

and back of this the top should be nailed fast. On the back 1 foot of 1-inch wire mesh should be stretched across the upper third and the lower two-thirds should be boarded up as shown in Fig. 1. There should be a box of dry grass or straw for the mink to hide in.

A larger "farm" may be a fenced-in yard of some 20 to 40 feet square, divided by inside fences into pens 10 to 20 feet wide and running the full length of the yard.

A stream or pond is not absolutely necessary, but it would be an advantage to have a small stream running across the pens as shown in Fig. 2.

The mink must have plenty of fresh water daily, and if they are kept as shown in Fig. 1, it should be given them in a granite pan about 3 inches deep and a foot square.

If there is no stream for the farm, the water may be run from a spring or other source into a trough of wood or concrete, or into a concrete well 2 or 3 feet deep in each yard. (See Fig. 2.)

The mink are happier with a stream, for they delight to play in the water, and the happier mink can be kept the better quality of fur may be marketed.

A plot of from one to five acres, containing a small pond or stream, with some shade, would make an ideal mink farm if it were not for the initial cost of fencing such an area.

The outside of the fence, shown in Fig. 2, should be built of 6 or 7-foot chestnut posts set 4 or 5 feet apart and 2 feet deep in a concrete wall. This wall is made by digging a trench 18 inches wide and 2 feet deep all around the inside of the yard, or the 1-inch mesh net may be extended 3 or 4 feet below the surface. A strip of 18 gauge 1-inch mesh 2 feet wide should be nailed to the posts, next to the foundation, and above that a strip of sheet-iron (12x3 ft.)

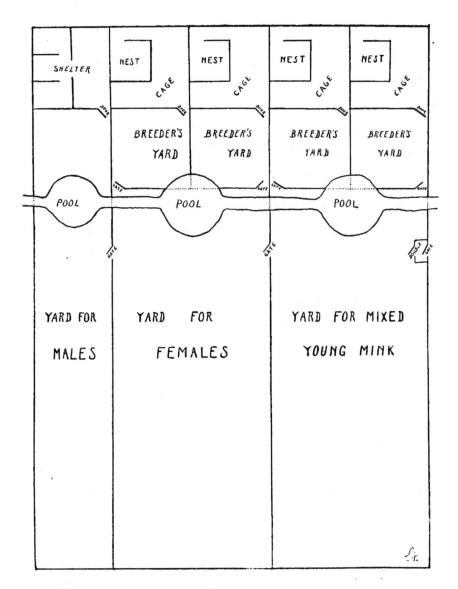

Fig. 2

should be nailed, leaving a 1-foot strip to be bent in for an "overhang." Angle-irons should be nailed or bolted to the posts, as shown in Fig. 3, and the sheet-iron bent over and fastened to them.

Or the entire fence may be of the netting, with "T" strips across the top of each post, on which a strip of netting is nailed for an overhang.

The higher your fence the safer your mink are from dogs getting in from outside, and a "T" or double overhang will prevent anything from climbing over the fence either way. Do not make the mistake of building your yards of boards, and allowing your valuable animals to escape.

The division fences may be of 1-inch mesh, with half of a sheet-iron strip nailed flat across the top to act as an overhang to keep the mink from climbing from one yard to the other. Gates should be made as in Fig. 2.

The nests may be boxes with hinged lids about a foot square and 6 inches to a foot high, placed as shown in Fig. 2, so that the round 5-inch opening to the nest will be more secluded and will not admit much light. The mother mink will like her nest much better this way, and if the young are not handled she will leave them in the nest till they are able to run about of themselves. A quantity of fine dried grass should be given for nests.

The individual cage in which the female is put for breeding should be 3 to 5 feet square and 4 feet deep at the front, or side next to the yard, and should have a board cover, hinged at the front and sloping toward the back to allow the water to run off.

These boards should be covered with tar-paper to exclude rain, for, although the mink is fond of water, it dislikes a damp, cold nest. The floor of the cage should also

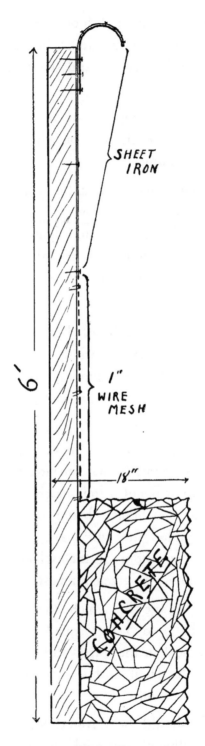

SHEET
IRON

6'

1"
WIRE
MESH

18"

CONCRETE

Fig. 3

be raised an inch or two above the ground on account of the dampness.

Road dust, sand or dry earth should be thrown over the cage floor, and this must be taken up and renewed every week. Keep a good supply on hand for this purpose.

In front of the cage should be the cage yard, containing a water trough and a feed pan. This yard is for the use of the female while rearing her young.

The large yards are for the mink between the breeding seasons, and for the young mink, if any, as indicated in Fig. 2. One yard is for mixed young mink, another for females, and a third, smaller yard, for the adult male or males. In each yard a shelter of boards covered with a foot or more of earth makes a cool retreat for the mink in summer. Plenty of shade MUST be provided if you wish to keep the fur dark, but there must be no boards or bushes near the fence so that the mink may climb out. Such a "farm" would probably cost from $50 to $100.

CHAPTER IV.

STOCKING THE FARM

Having made the yards ready, we will now consider how to procure the mink for breeding: Trapping the adult mink in the fall or winter, trapping or digging out the young mink in late April or in May, and also buying the mink from a dealer in animals or from a mink breeder.

Trapping seems to be preferable, for breeding mink are expensive animals to purchase. No one likes to part with a good breeding female for $25 when she is apt to bring her owner from 6 to 8 young ones, the pelts of which, if sold the following December, would bring between $50 and $75. That is why you are advised to begin as soon as possible and be ready to furnish breeders when the big demand comes.

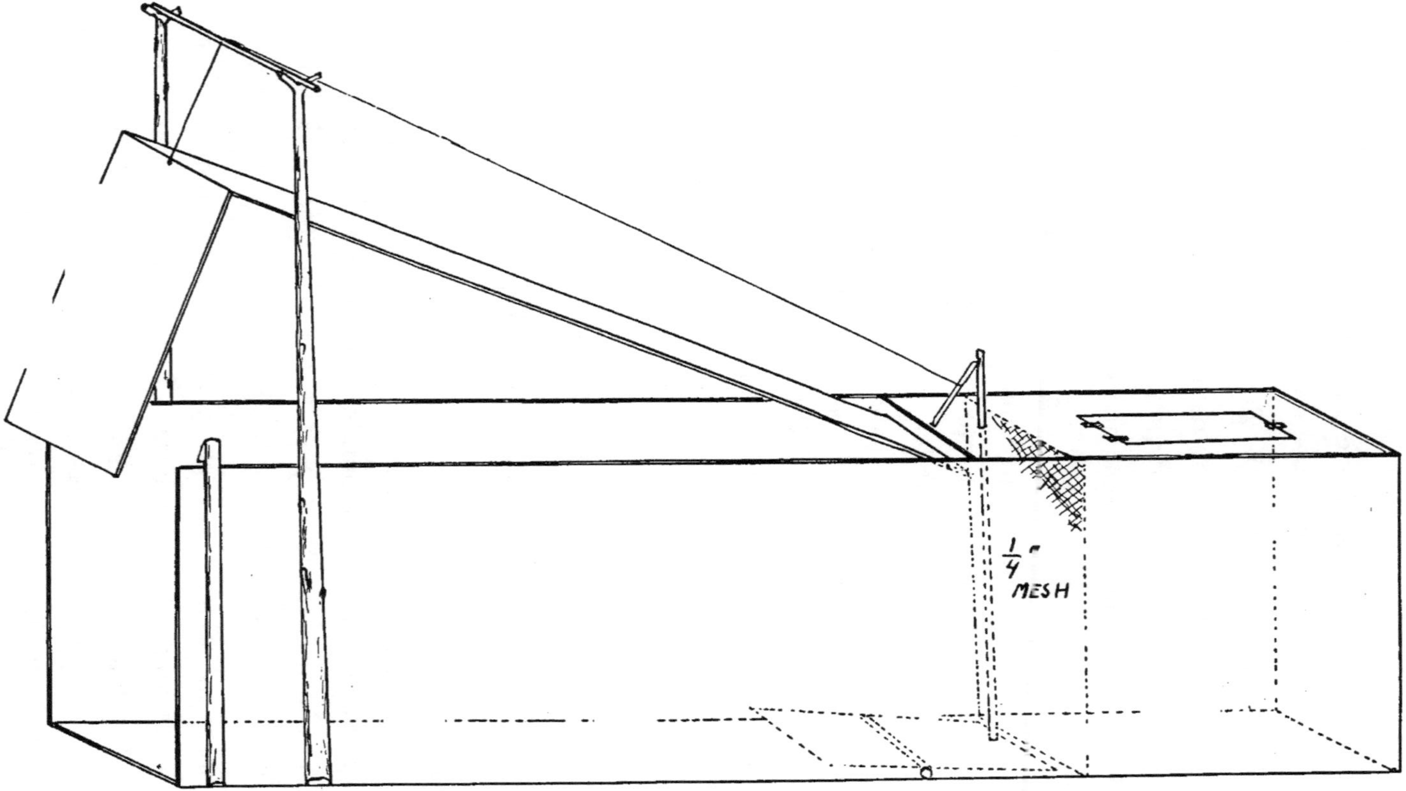

$\frac{1}{4}''$ MESH

Fig. 4

It pays to raise stock for breeding, as shown in the black fox industry of Canada, where Prince Edward Island farmers paid $10,000 a pair for breeding foxes the past summer.

The best trap for catching mink is the live-bait box-trap, baited with an old hen or two or three mice. The live bait is placed in a separate compartment at the back of the box-trap, so that the mink may see and smell them, but cannot harm them.

A quarter-inch mesh makes a good partition, and the mink, walking on a trip-pan, springs the trap.

The inside of the trap should clear from 2 feet to 30 inches in order to avoid injuring the mink in the door. The live-bait box-trap (Fig. 4) is one of the best I have used for catching mink.

It is better, on a small farm, to stock the mink in the fall, just after the ground is well frozen, for they will dig as deep as 3 feet in their attempts to get out. After three or four months they will give up such attempts for freedom and accept the farm as their home.

If they are captured in the fall they will have become reconciled to their new life by the time the ground is soft enough to dig into.

The mink born on the farm do not try to dig out. They will jump and climb, however, almost as well as a cat, and must be given no chance to get up on bushes or boards near the fence.

CHAPTER V.

BREEDING

The mink do not pair in captivity, and one male should be kept for five or six females.

Mink begin to breed when one year old and continue to breed for six or more years.

Mink raised by W. G. Gates, Prichard, Idaho.

The male should be kept separated from the females, except during the mating time, from February 15 to March 15.

The young, which are born blind and bare about six weeks later, are from four to eight in number.

Shut the female out of the cage and with a stick examine for any dead young. If any are found remove with a stick, being careful to avoid leaving any human taint in the nest, for that might cause the female to carry her young about and result in their being killed from exposure.

When a month old the young mink may be taken away from the female and placed in a yard by themselves until ready for market or for mating.

CHAPTER VI.

FEEDING

As already stated, mink may be fed on corn-bread and milk, but if they are wild adult mink they will have to be taught to eat cornmeal mush by feeding at first a little meat in their milk and they will get enough of the milk with the meat to form a liking for it in a short time.

Cornmeal mush cooked with a little fresh butchers' lean meat waste is the best all-round food as a steady diet. Fresh plucked sparrows or fresh fish may be given every four or five days.

The mink being a night-roamer, should be fed in the afternoon or evening, and only once a day, for if the food were given in the forenoon it would probably lie unheeded until night, when it would be too dry or spoiled.

In the morning take up what food is left uneaten. Use no salt, but give plenty of fresh water every day.

Females with sucking young should be fed twice daily. Keep everything clean and give only as much food as the mink will eat up at one feeding.

If the mink get too fat they become heated, shed their hair, lose their "prime" and develop poor fur. It is a good plan to let fat mink go without food every 15 days and it will do them good.

Mink may be fed as one does house cats, scraps from the table, johnny-cake and occasionally raw liver, but cooked food is the safe food, and one should not experiment on high-grade mink. (If you wish to experiment on feeding, select two or three scrub mink and try it on them.)

Wild mink eat frogs, but in my experience only a very hungry captive mink will eat a frog, and the frog must be a lively one.

Chicken heads and lights may be given occasionally if they are fresh. If possible, keep a cow for milk, raise corn for cornmeal mush. Enclose a one to five-acre swale with poultry netting and raise Belgian hares for mink food. There is nothing better in the meat line for mink than the blood and flesh of fresh killed rabbits, and a little may be given every day or two if you have enough to make it a regular practice. Stock a small pond with carp and have a supply of fresh fish on hand.

When all the food has to be purchased it costs about $2.50 to raise a mink to marketable age.

Just before killing time give the "prime" mink an egg every other day for a week and note the gloss on the pelt.

Remember that a happy and contented mink grows a prime pelt.

CHAPTER VII.

TAMING

The writer has found it impracticable to try to tame wild adult mink, but if handled with thick buckskin gloves the young born in captivity soon grow tame enough to be handled with the bare hands.

To take up a mink, move slowly and gently, placing the gloved hand, palm down, just over the mink's shoulder, pass the thumb and first finger around the neck. Be sure to HOLD the mink, for every failure makes him more difficult to tame. When you have hold of the mink, lift him up with one hand and with the other hold his hind legs.

If it is a young one and your gloves are thick, give him a chance to bite your finger, and when he does so pull toward the back of his mouth as you would pull on a gun trigger and his tusks will slip off the finger.

The harder you pull toward the hinge of his jaw the more sorry Mr. Mink will grow. If he squeals he may be (and usually is) conquered; if not, and he takes hold again, punish in the same way once more.

Tame mink bring big prices as pets and for breeding purposes. Female mink with young cannot be trusted as pets until after the young are weaned.

CHAPTER VIII.

MARKETING

Some time in October or November decide on which of the young females you wish to keep for breeding and put them in with the adult females.

It is not advisable to keep the young males unless you have a particularly fine dark one, but it is much better to get a new male occasionally, which can be done by exchanging your young males with other mink farmers or by trapping wild ones.

An Idaho mink breeder wrote me in March, 1913, as follows: "I am sold down to my breeding stock and have no more to spare. While they lasted I got $25 apiece for mink and sold three marten for $100."

If you have decided to kill some of the mink for market, feed them all they will eat (including eggs if they are not too costly) and when the pelts are prime, about December 15 to 20, usually after two or three weeks of severe cold weather, they will be fit to kill.

When the females are about seven years old they have reached their limit of usefulness and should be included in the lot prepared for market.

Prepare the skins according to the following directions and they may be kept till the market price is the highest.

CHAPTER IX.

SKINNING

To skin the mink, slit the legs on the under side from one foot across the vent to the other foot. Skin the legs, feet and toes, leaving the claws on the skin. Skin around the tail-bone, leaving the tail fast to the back of the skin, and pull the tail-bone out of the tail with the help of a split stick. Slit end of tail.

Then turn the skin over the body as if you were removing a shirt. Where necessary to start the skin use a knife, but be careful not to cut the skin nor leave any more flesh and fat on the skin than can be helped.

When you reach the front legs, slit the sole of the foot, skin and push them out whole, leaving the feet and toes on the skin. Next will come the ears, and they should be cut off close to the skull. Skin very carefully around the eyes, paying particular attention not to cut the eyelids, and follow on to the nose, leaving the pelt entire.

It is not considered a complete pelt unless the tail, feet and toes, ears, etc., are left on the skin.

Take off all extra flesh and fat and the skin is ready for the drying-board.

This drying-board should be about $2\frac{1}{2}$ feet long by about $4\frac{1}{2}$ inches wide at the bottom, tapering as shown in Fig. 5.

Pull the skin on the board with the belly on one side and the back on the other, with the fur side in, and stretch it snugly on the board so there are no wrinkles in the skin and the skin lies flat.

Tack it at the bottom on one side, and before tacking the other, run a smooth stick, the size of your finger, under the skin the length of the board. Have these sticks prepared, one for each board.

Put the skin in a dry, airy place where the sun cannot get at it, and never use artificial heat. A trifle of salt sprinkled into the tail after the tail-bone is removed is the only place where salt should be used.

When the skin is dry, pull out the stick and the skin will easily come off the board.

Do not use anything like salt or alum on the skin, as that may cause it to absorb moisture later, which may rot the skin.

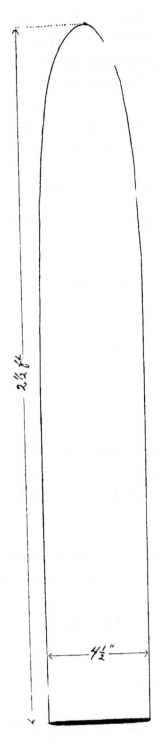

Fig. 5

CHAPTER X.

SHIPPING

Lay the skins out flat, cover them with paper and do them up in burlap, with your name and address on a card inside for identification, and if your skins are surely dry they are ready to ship.

Select a reliable dealer and write him what skins you are sending him, and how many. Put "From" and your name and address on the outside, as well as the name and address of the dealer to whom you ship your goods, and send them by parcels post.

IN CONCLUSION

Mink raising is not a "get-rich-quick" scheme, and those who cannot give the proper care and attention to the business had better close this book and forget it. Raise a pair of mink as a side issue for a year to become familiar with them, and put your book knowledge into practical experience. Above all, if you do not like pets, don't undertake fur breeding of any description. For the man or woman who goes into mink farming gradually and handles them intelligently there is a very comfortable, pleasant and remunerative business awaiting.

At present the following States do not prohibit, but encourage the raising and sale of mink:

Alabama, Arizona, Arkansas, California, Colorado, Connecticut, Georgia, Idaho, Indiana, Kentucky, Louisiana, Maine, Nebraska, New Hampshire, New Mexico, Ohio, Oklahoma, Oregon, Pennsylvania, Tennessee, Texas, Utah, Vermont, Virginia, West Virginia and Wisconsin.

In the following States one must obtain a permit or license:

Kansas, Maryland, Massachusetts, Michigan, Missouri, New Jersey and South Dakota.

The following States, at the present writing, prohibit mink raising, but it is indicated that they will soon pass laws favorable to game and fur breeders:

Florida, Iowa, Minnesota and New York.

Where the game laws conflict with mink raising, they were in force before raising mink as a business was considered.

It is advisable to consult the State Game Warden, enclosing a self-addressed and stamped envelope before engaging in mink breeding in any of the doubtful States.

Meanwhile the New York mink breeder may obtain one or more acres in Connecticut or New Jersey, within commuting distance, and engage in the mink business to any desired extent.

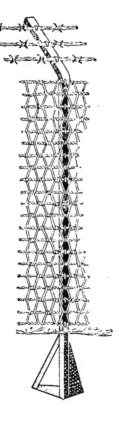

For non-climbable fences use a flea and mite proof steel fence post.

CARBO STEEL POSTS for maintaining sanitary conditions about your mink farm. All mink breeders endorse them. All users laud them.

Any kind of fencing easily and securely fastened. Use no concrete. No special tools. Ask for full information from

CARBO STEEL POST CO.

137½ TENTH ST.,

CHICAGO HEIGHTS,   ILLINOIS.

CPSIA information can be obtained
at www.ICGtesting.com
Printed in the USA
BVHW01s1122221217
503449BV00021B/710/P